Fish

FISH

Fish in the **ANIMAL WORLD**

Clown fish, a type of anemone fish, have brightly coloured bodies with white bands. They are known as anemone fish because of their symbiotic relationship with sea anemones.

Classification of fish

Fish have long colonized every expanse of water on earth, be it fresh or salt, cold, temperate or warm. These cold-blooded aquatic vertebrates inhabit everything from the smallest pond to the widest ocean. They come in so many shapes, colours and sizes that they almost defy classification.

Like sharks, rays have a cartilaginous skeleton rather than a bony one. Most of the 300 or so species have rather broad, flat, disc-shaped bodies.

It should be easy to define a fish as an aquatic animal which moves with the aid of fins, obtains oxygen by breathing water through its gills and has skin that is covered with scales. However, many fish do not fit this neat description. Some do not have scales, others have no fins and, instead, propel themselves through the water with weaving movements of their whole body. Some fish only have vestigial gills, breathing through lungs or other specialized organs which allow them to spend long periods out of water. All of this makes it

The mirror carp has only a few large scales. The leather carp has almost none!

At the beginning of the dry season, this Cameroonian lungfish hollows out a hole in the mud where it remains until the rains come, breathing through its two lungs.

The body of the boxfish is protected by a carapace, or shell, of bony plates. Its shape makes it a slow swimmer but it can perform an about-turn on the spot.

The pipefish, with its elongated body, does not look much like a fish at all.

very difficult to come up with a blanket description that works for all the 30,000 or so species designated by the term 'fish'.

Like a fish in water!

For a long time, the term 'fish' was used to refer to any animal living in water, including dolphins, mussels and crabs. Nowadays, we tend to think of fish as the members of a single group which scientists call the Teleosts and which numbers some 25,000 recorded species. However, even within this group, it can be a daunting task trying to

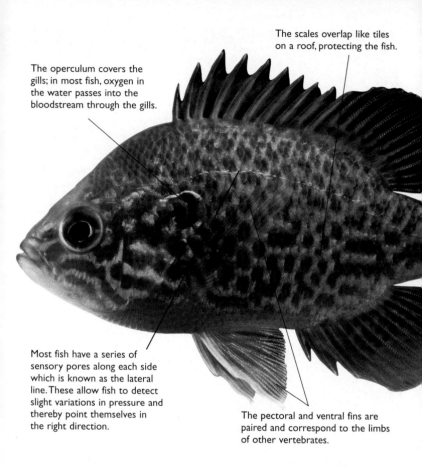

The scales overlap like tiles on a roof, protecting the fish.

The operculum covers the gills; in most fish, oxygen in the water passes into the bloodstream through the gills.

Most fish have a series of sensory pores along each side which is known as the lateral line. These allow fish to detect slight variations in pressure and thereby point themselves in the right direction.

The pectoral and ventral fins are paired and correspond to the limbs of other vertebrates.

▼ Naturalists classify fish according to external features such as the presence, number and position of fins, the colour, shape and type of scales and the presence and arrangement of the lateral line. It is usually possible to tell how a fish lives and to identify its natural environment from these different features. Strong fast swimmers (known as pelagic species), such as tuna, have a torpedo-shaped body, while slower swimmers (benthic species), such as the sole, tend to be flat and dwell on the bottom of seas or lakes. The least mobile often have spherical bodies, whilst fish living in the depths of the great oceans tend to have very deep flattened bodies.

identify what a pike, an eel and a sea horse have in common!

Trying to classify 30,000 species of fish

Some lines can be drawn on the basis of anatomy and the evolution of species and this makes it possible to distinguish fish with cartilaginous skeletons, such as sharks and rays, from those with bony skeletons. Bony fish are by far the larger of these two groups, including several species which first appeared in the distant past and whose descendants (the sturgeon, for example) retain certain primitive characteristics, such as a blowhole. Fish belonging to groups which have evolved more recently have developed their swim bladder, an amazing organ which was originally part of the respiratory system and which enables them to reduce or increase their specific gravity by absorbing or expelling air, thereby making it possible to move up or down in the water. However, anyone looking for a single scientific classification which encompasses all varieties of fish will be disappointed since different schools of thought cannot agree upon the way in which these strange animals should be categorized.

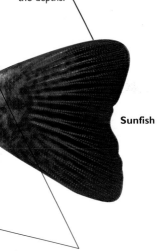

The tail, or caudal, fin is usually the main means of propulsion. The fish fills its swim bladder with air in order to rise towards the surface and empties it again when it wants to descend to the depths.

Sunfish

Like the tail fin, the dorsal and anal fins are unpaired. They are located on the median line of the back and underbelly.

The flounder is a bottom-dwelling fish with a flat body that allows it to bury itself in sand or soft mud. Both eyes are located on the top of its head.

Sea horses use their prehensile tails to hold on to seaweed.

Two different approaches

In an attempt to impose some sort of order upon the varied world of fish, exponents of the phenetic system of taxonomic classification (from the Greek *phenos*, meaning 'appearance') create enormous data banks which are used to make minute comparisons of characteristics to see whether they are shared by different species. The cladists (from the Greek *klados*, meaning 'branch') claim that this is a superficial approach. They prefer to classify plants and animals in phyla based on their evolutionary history.

In the murky depths of the ocean, the deep-sea angler fish moves its luminous antenna like a lure to attract prey towards its enormous gaping mouth.

Evidence dating from the Eocene Epoch, some 35 to 54 million years ago, suggests that fish already looked much as they do today and that some also swam in shoals.

The cladists believe that many animals do present similarities but that these have more to do with their adaptation to a specific environment (in this case, water) than with any real kinship.

Strange relatives

The first vertebrates to inhabit the earth developed in water. Some then moved on to dry land and evolved into the terrestrial classes (amphibians, reptiles, birds and mammals), whilst others evolved exclusively in water. From a strictly cladist or genealogical point of view, the

Some say the coelacanth is more closely related to the rhinoceros than the trout!

The coelacanth has hardly changed for several million years. Its most recent descendants, such as this *Latimeria chalumnae*, tend to be found in the Indian Ocean.

coelacanth and other lunged fish are therefore more closely related to the sparrow and the elephant than to the salmon or the trout! Cladists would argue that there is little point in giving the name 'fish' to creatures descended from different classes. Most biologists, however, do not subscribe to revolutionary ideas of this kind. The rhinoceros is certainly descended from the same class as the coelacanth, but while the rhino is the end product of an extremely rapid process of evolution, the coelacanth has scarcely changed for 350 million years. It looks, behaves and tastes like a fish. Would it really seem logical to call it anything else?

From the rivers of Africa...

A world of infinite variety

These contradictory theories are a telling reflection of the complexity of the fish world. Each of the various methods of classification attaches particular importance to certain characteristics of fish, be it the evolution of the species or the adaptation to a particular environment. One thing is clear – that the world at the bottom of the ocean, filled with nomads, predators and masters of disguise, is a truly fascinating one.

...to the lakes of Scandinavia, freshwater fish are found all over the planet.

▼ At least 4000 species of fish inhabit the world's coral reefs. These biotopes (regions that are uniform in environmental conditions), where the water is very warm, are like oases in the middle of a desert formed by the surrounding ocean. In addition to their more permanent inhabitants, coral reefs also attract a great many migratory fish. A single reef may be inhabited by over 200 different species. Most reef-dwellers, such as the white-bellied surgeonfish, are brightly coloured and spend the day near the surface.

The colour and shape of the stonefish give it the appearance of an algae-encrusted rock. This pitiless hunter waits, motionless, for its next victim.

Masters of disguise

The struggle for survival is as fierce in the water as it is on land and, for many, the key to survival is camouflage. For the inhabitants of the sea, it is better to hide than be eaten...and much easier to capture prey if your victim does not spot you first!

This stargazer lies buried in the sand in the coastal waters of the Mediterranean, waiting for its prey. Only its bulging eyes and large mouth can be seen.

The slogan for a famous road safety campaign once ran: Be seen, Be safe. Many species of animal, however, adopt quite a different maxim and assure their safety by not being seen. Fish are no exception. Most fish camouflage themselves by blending in with their environment. For this reason, cold-water fish tend to be brown or greenish in colour, but more surprising perhaps are the rainbow hues of the fish that live in warm seas. They too have adapted to their surroundings, living as they do among brightly coloured coral reefs.

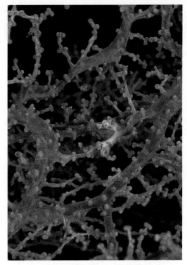

Who goes there? This gorgon seahorse displays its powers of camouflage.

The markings of the coral grouper are perfectly adapted to its environment. This sharp-toothed carnivore inhabits the coastal reefs of the Pacific Ocean.

The pikeperch lives in fresh or slightly salt water. As its colouring suggests, it prefers the shallow murky waters of river estuaries to the clear running water of streams.

Surgeonfish can change their bright colours to suit their surroundings.

A colour to suit every environment

Far below the surface of the Mediterranean, a scorpion fish lying in wait for prey on a rock is almost invisible, as is a perch or tench lurking in the green waters of a river. There are a whole range of markings to suit every environment: silvery blue-grey for fish which swim in open water, various shades of mottled grey for those living on sandy or gravelly bottoms, speckled dark brown for rocky surroundings and a whole range of greens for fish living among water plants.

Water chameleons

The sole is the undisputed master of disguise, changing colour to blend in with any environment. Its skin contains small pigment cells, or chromatophores, which can change the colour of the skin simply by expanding or contracting. And the sole is not alone...if you put a plaice on a chessboard, it will reproduce the squares of the board on its own skin!

Appearances can be deceptive

The butterfly fish has markings which resemble an eye (known as an ocellus) near its tail, while its real eyes are masked by stripes. Predators are often fooled into thinking that they are attacking the head, which is the most vulnerable part of a fish, when in fact they are attacking the tail. It would seem logical that these markings are there for the purpose of self-preservation, but the theory has never been proven. Studies of this fish's behaviour have only served to reveal other stratagems: its deep flattened body allows it to slip into the narrowest crevices if pursued and, when trapped, it lowers its head and raises its dorsal spines in order to intimidate the enemy.

The speckled garden eel retreats into the sand at the least sign of danger.

Manini surgeonfish swim alone or in shoals and feed on the algae that grow on coral. Their markings are perfectly adapted to their habitat.

▼ Camouflage is not only useful when it comes to escaping predators. It is also an excellent resource when hunting. The finest example of this is given by the angler fish. Resembling a seaweed-covered rock, it is a master of the surprise attack. Patiently waiting for its prey, it remains perfectly motionless except for the slight movement of a tiny antenna above its head. When a creature approaches, attracted by the antenna which it has mistaken for a worm, all the angler fish has to do is open its enormous mouth and swallow the hapless victim.

Coral reefs are home to an enormous wealth of animal species. The dazzling colours of the coral are equalled only by those of the fish themselves.

Becoming invisible

The colour of many fish enables them to blend in with their environment. Other reef-dwelling species, however, employ an ingenious system of camouflage which relies upon a phenomenon known by scientists as 'disruptive colouring'. The markings of these fish are distributed in such a way as to draw the eye away from the outline of their bodies. From the point of view of survival, this gives them one distinct advantage: by having such an appearance, the fish look like a set of disparate shapes which are of no interest to predators.

From its hiding place, the moray eel is ready to pounce on passing prey.

With colourful markings, a deep flattened body which allows it to slip into narrow crevices, and stripes concealing its eyes, the butterfly fish is perfectly adapted to life among the coral.

The lionfish is one of the strangest inhabitants of the coral reef. Its dorsal fin has spines which are connected to poison glands.

▼ Rock-dwelling fish do not have a monopoly on camouflage. Species which live in open water, such as these jacks which shoal to the south-east of the Bahamas, are also camouflaged by their skin colouring. The top part of their body is dark blue and the lower part silver. This means that when seen from above the fish merge into the blue depths of the water and when seen from below the metallic glint of their underbellies could be mistaken for sun rays reflecting off the surface of the water. At least by would-be predators...

Incorrigible squatters

Moray eels hide in holes in the rock so that they can watch for prey, but, when it comes to ingenious hidey-holes, the prize must surely go to the pearl fish that takes up residence inside a living sea cucumber! Its small slender body is adapted to this strange habitat where it spends most of its life. It only leaves its host to go in search of food and returns to the refuge at the slightest sign of danger.

These catfish huddle together to discourage would-be aggressors.

When you can't see the wood for the trees

Strange as it may seem, the sight of a shoal of fish does not necessarily attract the attention of potential enemies. Many small fish swim in shoals as a means of escaping their larger predators. Anchovies and sardines are prime examples of fish that have understood the advantages of a group existence and always swim in shoals. When a mackerel, barracuda or tuna shows a little too much interest, the small fish close ranks, making it virtually impossible for the predator to target or even make out one particular victim in the mass of moving bodies. The larger fish is often forced to retreat hungry. Proof indeed that, even in the fish world, there is safety in numbers.

Like many fish, *Sebastes marinus* travels great distances at different periods of its life. It is found in the North Atlantic between the coasts of Norway and Newfoundland.

Nomads and travellers

Many fish, such as tuna, eels and, of course, salmon, migrate during their lifetime, from north to south, from the coast to the open seas or even from the depths of the ocean to its surface. They travel several thousand kilometres on a journey that sometimes costs them their lives...

A salmon can travel upstream at a speed of 1 metre per second against a current moving at 6 metres per second. Each leap can be as high as 3 metres and as long as 5 metres.

N orth-Sea fishermen have long been aware that herrings do not remain in one place all year round, but move in enormous shoals according to the season, each shoal following its own route. Fish that spawn off Scotland in summer subsequently migrate towards south-west Norway while those that breed off Dunkirk and Fécamp in February spend the summer in the central and northern part of the North Sea. The main reason for these constant migrations lies in the seasonal variation in the temperature and salinity of the water. Herring need cold water and low levels of salt in order to survive. By travelling such long distances, they are simply seeking out the fluctuations in salinity and temperature which suit them best.

The tuna is one of the ocean's greatest migrators, attaining incredible speeds on its journeys. In order to move through the water as quickly as possible, it folds its pectoral and dorsal fins against its body to make itself more streamlined.

Salmon could once be found swimming upstream in almost all European rivers. However, the creation of dams and the even more serious problem of water pollution have forced them to take refuge in more remote areas.

Unlike the herring of the North Sea and the Atlantic Ocean, those in the Pacific are more sedentary and do not migrate long distances.

In summer, tightly packed shoals of anchovies inhabit coastal waters.

A tireless swimmer

It was also with the help of fishermen that, back in the 1920s, an Italian zoologist was able to plot the migratory route of the red tuna. Tuna caught in the Mediterranean were found to have Portuguese fish hooks from the Azores and American ones from Massachusetts in their mouths, as well as the marks of Norwegian harpoons on their bodies. By tagging tuna, it has also been possible to calculate the speed at which they travel. Some tagged fish covered 9200 kilometres in 50 days, the equivalent of 184 kilometres a

Young plumed jacks live near the surface of the water, but, when fully grown, prefer to descend to depths of over 60 m. Their narrow flattened bodies make them fast swimmers.

▼ A great deal of research has been carried out into the migration of fish. In order to plot their routes, scientists mark the fish by fixing plastic tags to one of their fins or gill covers. For smaller fish, metal plates are introduced into their stomachs. When the fish are caught again, these tags and metal plates, indicating where the fish were caught the first time, enable their migrations to be traced. In the case of the smaller fish, which are often ground up to make fishmeal, the metal plates are recovered in factories by powerful magnets.

The spindle-shaped body of the blue marlin enables it to reach high speeds.

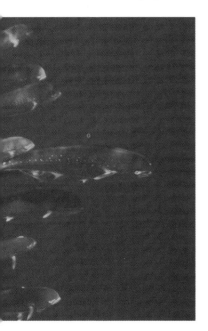

day! These large fish breed in the Mediterranean and are weak and hungry by the time they leave the spawning grounds in July and August, bound for the North Atlantic where there are garfish, mackerel and herring in abundance. Having eaten their fill, they then head for warmer waters as soon as the temperature of the North Atlantic drops. These powerful fish do not like swimming in water which is less than 14°C (57°F) and must maintain a body temperature of 22°C (70°F).

Back to square one

The salmon starts life in the clear waters of small rivers and mountain streams, but it is only as it matures and turns silver that the real adventure begins. When this happens, the fish's thyroid gland secretes a hormone with a high iodine content into the bloodstream, stimulating the young salmon, which lets itself be carried downstream. When it reaches the sea, the sodium in the salt water neutralizes the effect of the iodine. The salmon measures between 10 and 20 centimetres at this point but grows rapidly as it journeys around the Atlantic or Pacific before retracing its steps to its original spawning grounds.

During the period when salmon are swimming upstream in Canadian rivers, bears appear on the river banks to catch the fish 'in flight'. Some eat up to 15 salmon a day.

Fatal feats

The fat reserves laid down by salmon during their time in the sea provide the energy for the journey back through fresh water. Navigating using their sense of smell, the fish are able to identify the water in which they spent their early lives, even though it has been greatly diluted. As they swim back upstream, they stop feeding. Exhausted, the survivors arrive at the place where they were spawned...at which point, the males must summon up all their remaining energy in order to fight for a female before spawning in their turn.

The silver colour of a salmon changes as it leaves the sea and returns upstream.

Swimming side by side with their mouths open, the male and female salmon deposit the milt (sperm) and roe (eggs) in a trench previously hollowed out by the female.

Destination unknown

Unlike salmon, the European eel (*Anguilla anguilla*) starts life in the extremely salty waters of the Sargasso Sea, north-east of the Antilles. The eel larvae are borne along by the warm waters of the Gulf Stream, taking more than three years to reach the shores of Europe. Here, they metamorphose into elvers, or 'glass eels', and begin their journey upstream. Once in the river, they begin a period of growth (females can reach a length of up to 1.5 metres), lay down fat reserves and change colour, becoming 'yellow eels'. After about ten years in

Like many other fish, the cod migrates in order to feed and spawn.

During its time in the ocean, the salmon finds its way around by means of an 'internal clock' and by using the position of the sun, rather like a sailor taking bearings.

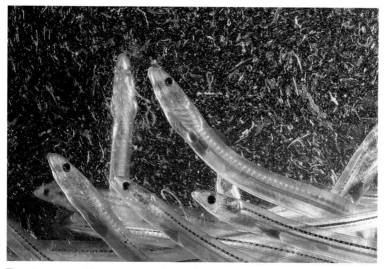

The transparent eel larvae turn into elvers when they reach the coasts of Europe. As elvers, their skin takes on a darker colour.

fresh water, eels undergo a strange metamorphosis: their heads become pointed, their eyes grow larger and their bodies turn darker and develop silvery markings. Soon they stop feeding and, under the cover of darkness, set off for the open sea. It is then that all trace of them disappears! Do they return to the Sargasso Sea, swimming at great depths, in order to spawn in their turn? Or is the new generation of European eels born of American eels? The whole subject remains a mystery: an adult European eel has never been caught in the Atlantic.

On its journey upstream, the yellow eel may even crawl across meadows.

Although it poses no threat to humans, the pike is a fearsome predator. The female is larger than the male and can measure 1.5 m in length and weigh as much as 45 kilos!

Natural-born killers

The tales of mariners, gory news items
and horror films constantly remind us
of the blood-thirsty hunters that lurk
within the waters of our planet: great whites, tiger
sharks, giant rays, barracuda in the tropics, piranhas
in the Amazon Basin and even pike in our own rivers.

The tiger shark is the most dangerous inhabitant of the tropical seas. It feeds mainly on
seabirds, turtles, porcupine fish, rays...and other sharks.

A mong all the species of fish, it is mention of the shark that conjures up the image of a terrifying creature ready to snap up some hapless swimmer in its powerful jaws or take off a limb with one bite. This reputation is not entirely unjustified, particularly in tropical waters where most of the world's man-eating sharks live. In reality, however, only about 20 of the 300 or so known species of shark are actually of any danger to humans. The whale shark and the basking shark, the two largest fish in the world, are in actual fact gentle giants that feed on

A third of all human deaths caused by sharks are attributed to the great white.

Carpet sharks live on the bottom of fairly shallow tropical and subtropical seas. Their skin has outgrowths which resemble seaweed and provide them with perfect camouflage.

The grey shark is an inquisitive creature by nature and can be a danger to divers.
It sways to and fro on the spot in a threatening manner before attacking.

The hammerhead shark owes its name to the fleshy extensions on either side of its head. Its eyes can be up to a metre apart!

plankton at the surface of the water. However, as far as other fish are concerned, most sharks are indeed fierce predators.

The smell of blood

Although their hunting techniques vary, all sharks use their sense of smell to track prey. The larger species, which hunt alone, can detect blood in the water more than a kilometre away. It comes as no surprise, therefore, to learn that two thirds of a shark's brain are dedicated to the sense of smell. Vibrations detected by the nerves in the

This set of jaws from a tiger shark makes a spectacular hunting trophy.

lateral line also guide the hunter towards its victim which it then normally swims round or warily approaches. If a shark is hungry, however, it can rush upon its prey at speeds of up to 80 km/h! Sight plays a much less important role in these attacks, with moving objects being distinguished more by reflection than by colour.

A terrifying set of teeth

Large sharks, such as the great white or the tiger shark, are able to tear off enormous chunks of flesh with one bite and swallow them without chewing. The rows

The shark's torpedo-shaped body means it can attack at great speed.

of triangular teeth with their jagged edges can easily take off a person's leg or shear through skin as hard and thick as that of a crocodile! The teeth of the great blue shark are honed to such a sharp edge that the Maoris of New Zealand use them as razors. With teeth like that, the shark lives in fear of few predators. Although some large species, particularly the great white, regularly attack humans (11 people were killed in 1997), the latter are as equally predatory. These large fish are hunted not only to remove a potential danger from coastal areas, but also for their meat which is highly prized; shark steaks are eaten all over the world and the Chinese have, since ancient times, used the dorsal fin as the basis of a particular type of soup. In Australia, where over the past few decades less than one person per year has been victim of a shark attack, there are so few great whites left that they are now a protected species.

The leopard shark is a solitary creature which feeds on molluscs and small fish.

The barracuda: a fish with an enquiring mind...

Many tropical divers fear the barracuda more than they do the shark due to the fact that this predator with its smooth

The guitarfish has a flattened upper body, rather like a ray. This strange fish has a long tail which enables it to make sudden movements.

▼ The manta ray, or devilfish, (opposite) can grow to a width of over 7 metres. Its huge mouth engulfs small crustaceans and fish which are filtered out by sieve-like gill slits. Other rays make up for their inability to move quickly by expelling a powerful jet of water which blasts a crater in the seabed, revealing small creatures and plankton. At the end of a day's hunting for food, these craters, which may be up to 50 centimetres deep and 1.5 metres wide, can cover a surface area of up to 10 km^2.

During the day, most barracuda swim in shoals. Most species live in subtropical coastal waters and migrate to temperate seas during the summer.

Unlike sharks, barracuda only attack once, but their enormous mouths, bristling with pointed teeth, are capable of wreaking terrible damage upon their victims.

elongated body, pointed head, projecting lower jaw and fang-like teeth likes to follow them...very closely indeed. Such fears appear to be largely groundless, however, since only about forty attacks by this highly inquisitive fish have ever been recorded.

...and an insatiable appetite

Barracuda are excellent swimmers; they are attracted by colour and movement and use their eyes to locate prey. Young barracuda hunt in packs and, once

Barracuda are joined among the reefs by other predators, such as this lemon shark.

The honeycomb moray is so called on account of its regular honeycomb markings. This large 'sea snake' can reach up to 3 metres in length!

▼ Congers, any of around 100 species of marine eels, are the 'cosmopolitan' cousins of the morays, widely found along the rocky coasts of all tropical and subtropical seas. The European conger eel (Conger conger) is one of the largest, growing to a length of more than 2 metres. It is a carnivorous creature, using its strong teeth to devour crustaceans as well as fish, octopus and certain varieties of mussel. It is thought that conger eels spawn in the open seas at a depth of around 2500 metres, then die soon after.

they have detected a school of small fish, attack swiftly and devour victim after victim until they are sated. Barracuda which have just eaten their fill have even been known to herd survivors into a shallow spot so that they can be captured more easily at the next mealtime.

The serpents of the sea

Morays and conger eels are also endowed with sharp teeth and an ability to swim at great speed. Their powerful, scaleless, snake-like bodies make them incredibly agile, while their sharp teeth, which are often arranged in several rows, cut effortlessly through the flesh of their victims. Morays also inject poison when they bite and in five species this poison can be fatal to humans. They generally feed on fish, but can easily crush mussels and shellfish in their powerful jaws.

Morays: twilight hunters

The zebra moray of the Indian Ocean is a fairly harmless creature.

During the day, morays hide in crevices and cavities around the rocky coasts and coral reefs that they inhabit, emerging only at dusk to go hunting. They do, however, remain on their guard and will react aggressively at any time, so beware of sticking your hand into a hole in search of some hidden treasure! Despite their fearsome teeth, morays have been prized as food since ancient times. To avoid any danger of being poisoned, fishermen cut off the eels' heads as soon as they are caught.

The pike: a freshwater barracuda

Freshwater predators can be pretty fierce too. Although the pike does not have the stamina of its marine counterparts to cover long distances, it is a champion

The pike uses its excellent eyesight to locate prey.

Like a tiger waiting for its victim in long grass, the pike hides itself in the thick vegetation which grows underwater at the edge of rivers.

As soon as it is 3 or 4 centimetres long, the young pike abandons its diet of plankton in favour of small fish.

sprinter which waits, hidden in the waterweed where it is perfectly camouflaged, for the right moment to attack. It uses its eyes and lateral line to locate prey, lunging at its victim and swallowing it whole. A meal can sometimes take several days to digest...

An indiscriminate glutton

The basic diet of the adult pike consists mainly of fish and insects, but it will not turn its nose up at frogs, voles and birds which venture imprudently to the water's

The pike's enormous mouth is an indication of the size of its appetite.

edge. The bigger the victim the better, as far as the pike is concerned, since it expends less energy in attacking one large victim than it would in catching several smaller ones. However, this greed can prove fatal. It is not unusual to find a pike which has choked to death, its prey still in its mouth...

Piranhas: the terror of the Amazon Basin

Just one of the thousands of stories which are told about the terrible piranha fish of the Amazon Basin recounts that a man on horseback was attacked while crossing a river; all that was found were the man's clothes, his skeleton and that of his horse. These small carnivorous fish of the genus *Serrasalmus* are attracted to movement as well as to the slightest drop of blood in the water. They make up for their modest size (most measuring between 20 and 30 centimetres in length) by having strong jaws that bear razor-sharp teeth. Hunting in packs of several hundred, they are capable of stripping a sizeable carcass to the bone in no time at all. During the rainy season, it is particularly dangerous to cross parts of a river where male piranhas are guarding the eggs.

The strong sharp teeth of the piranha close in a scissorlike bite.

According to some sources, schools of piranhas act as undertakers' assistants in flooded areas of the Orinoco delta, stripping the flesh off dead bodies.

▼ Sunfish are instantly recognizable by their variegated markings. They live in rivers, lakes, marshes and some European river estuaries where their large appetites can sometimes decimate populations of smaller species. The largest specimens are highly prized by fishers. Sunfish feed on fish as well as frogs, worms, small crustaceans and spawn. At the end of the 19th century, some non-European species were introduced to the rivers of Europe to enrich the local fauna but these quickly attacked the eggs and fry of other indigenous fish.

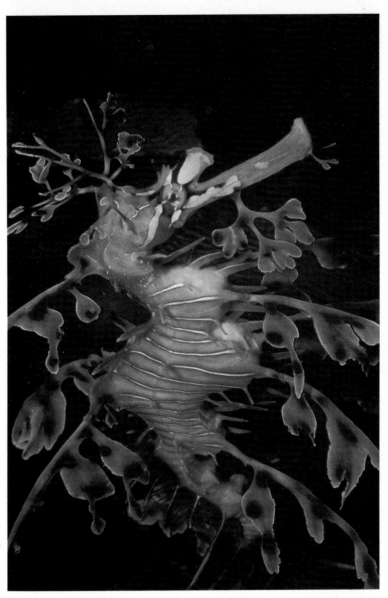

This sea dragon looks like a piece of floating seaweed. It is hard to recognize it as a fish unless you consider other criteria than just its appearance.

Weird and wonderful

There are more species of fish than there are amphibians, reptiles, birds and mammals put together, so it is hardly surprising that some of them should have strange habits, an odd appearance or a surprising lifestyle. Some of their unusual and exotic ways almost defy belief.

The lionfish uses its enormous pectoral fins as a net with which to capture prey in even the most tortuous crevices of the reef.

Names such as globe-fish, frogfish, lantern fish, drum fish, moon-fish, redfish, blackfish, flying fish and pilot fish are suggestive of the infinite variety of colours, shapes, lifestyles and particular characteristics that make up the vast and endlessly surprising world of fish.

Not so silent

Contrary to popular belief, fish do in fact make sounds. Some are even quite noisy, especially during the mating season. The repertoire of fish sounds includes tooting,

The multicoloured stripes of the rasbora.

Cartilaginous fish, such as sharks, have no swim bladder and must keep swimming so that they do not sink to the bottom.

The black-and-white drum fish makes sounds which are audible to humans by vibrating the skin of its swim bladder.

Frogfish can swallow prey as big as themselves.

chirping, clicking, rattling, humming and drumming. The grunt grinds its teeth to produce the sound that gave it its name. Amplified by the fish's swim bladder, the sound can be heard for many kilometres. The swim bladder is also used as a kind of sound box by members of the *Scienidae* family, to which the drum fish belongs. Through clever use of this organ, fish can generate a great deal of noise in the sea, as the American Navy discovered to its cost during World War II. When the Japanese were launching their surprise attack on the naval base at

This strange creature half-buried in the sand, with bony ridges all over its head, looks more like a crocodile than a fish. Its effective disguise makes it very difficult to see.

Blennies are bottom-dwelling fish, most of which have neither scales nor swim bladders. Seen from the front, they sometimes look more like toads than fish.

Pearl Harbor, the Americans mistook the throb of their submarine engines for the noise made by drum fish.

Fish on the wing

While trout and salmon are capable of spectacular leaps, the former to catch flies, the latter to clear rapids, members of the *Exocoetidae* family – better known as flying fish – can glide for several hundred metres over the sea using their enlarged pectoral fins like wings.

Is it a bird? Is it a plane? A flying fish in full flight above the ocean.

Tree fish!

In certain other species, the pectoral fins have developed into limbs. The sargassum fish, or frogfish, holds on to gulfweed with its 'hands' so that it does not sink to the bottom of the ocean with no hope of returning to the surface. Lungfish, on the other hand, crawl around on the seabed. The rockskipper (*Istiblennius zebra*), a small Hawaiian blenny, even ventures on to dry land. Mudskippers are so well adapted to their natural habitat in the mangrove swamps of Africa and Asia that they have developed pectoral fins which allow them to crawl or hop about on the mud...and even climb trees!

Scorpion fish have a predilection for very large prey.

Danger – poison!

Fins, however, are not just used by fish for getting about. Some also form part of their defence mechanism. The rays (the hard parts which form the framework of the fin) on the dorsal and pectoral fins of certain catfish are connected to poison glands. Similarly, scorpion fish off the rocky coasts of the Mediterranean and eastern Atlantic have fin spines that, although not always containing poison, can still be hazardous to swimmers, causing painful wounds if stepped on.

The greater weever is often found between Sweden and Denmark. Fishermen must handle it with care, removing the venomous spines from its dorsal fin.

▼ Glands connected to spines on the dorsal and anal fins of scorpion fish and stargazers secrete a deadly poison. The scorpion fish (of the genus Scorpaena) inhabits the rocky coasts of temperate and tropical seas where it lies in wait for prey, pouncing on its victim or simply opening its big mouth and sucking it in. The stargazer, meanwhile, hides in the sand, waiting for crustaceans and fish. During the course of its evolution, it has developed spade-like pectoral fins which it uses to dig or stir up the sand around itself.

Ouch!

Care should also be taken by those walking on sandy beaches, who may be in for a painful surprise if they tread on the sharp spines of weevers. The venom they contain destroys red blood cells, paralyses nerves and causes swellings. Still more treacherous  are certain puffer fish which remain poisonous even when dead. Despite the fact that some of their organs contain a highly toxic substance, they are eaten in Japan (where they are known as *fugu*), once the flesh has been carefully cleaned.

Porcupine fish inflate themselves and erect their spines in self-defence.

In addition to their spines, members of the *Diodontidae* family, such as this porcupine fish, have strong beaks, which enable them to crack open the shellfish that form their diet.

The scaleless skin of the common puffer fish is strong and elastic and allows the fish to inflate itself by swallowing water.

A poisonous football

If threatened, porcupine fish (related to puffers) erect the spines concealed in the pores of their skin or inflate themselves with water or air. These spines are not usually poisonous and specimens washed up on the banks of the Ubangi River in central Africa are used as balls by the local children. These fish live mostly near the coast although some varieties are river-dwellers. In order to eat, they squirt out a jet of water to uncover the crustaceans, mussels and sea snails that form their diet. Rapid movements of the dorsal and anal fin in either direction enable puffer fish to turn, rise or fall, rather like a helicopter.

The electric eel can generate 550 volts of electricity.

Strange habits

Fish also have some strange practices when it comes to reproduction. Some female groupers are able to turn themselves into males which are capable of reproducing. Other curiosities include the male stickleback which builds a nest for its eggs whereas most fish deposit their spawn in the water, the male sea horse, which keeps its eggs in a ventral pouch, and several species of catfish, which hatch their young in their mouths!

The marbled electric ray lives on the sandy bed of the eastern Atlantic, between France and South Africa, as well as in the Mediterranean. It can descend to depths of 250 m.

▼ If you touch an electric ray, such as the eyed variety pictured left, you will receive a powerful electric shock. Some of the muscles close to its head have developed into electrodes which are negative on the inside and positive on the outside. Once the ray has located its victim, it wraps its fins around it and gives it a violent electric shock. The pectoral fins cannot, therefore, be used for swimming, so electric rays use their ventral fins to 'walk' along the seabed where they hide in the sand, lying in wait for their prey.

Till death us do part

In some species of angler fish, the males are tiny (a few centimetres long) compared with females which can grow to a metre in length! This means that, in spite of the luminous organs they possess, the two sexes can have trouble finding each other. When they do eventually get together, the males attach themselves to the female like parasites, biting into her skin. Their mouths become fused with her skin and the two bloodstreams become interconnected. From then on, the males remain totally dependent on the female for nourishment.

The colour of this grouper changes according to its environment and mood!

Scaleless skin and two or three pairs of barbels are the distinctive features of the 2200 or so species of silurids (which include catfish), most of which live in fresh water.

The courtship dance performed by sea horses and pipefish is a veritable ballet during which the female deposits her eggs in the ventral pouch of the male.

Down at the bottom of the deep blue sea

For a long time, it was thought that nothing lived at the bottom of the world's oceans. The cold, darkness and tremendous pressure (which increases 1 kilogram per cubic centimetre every 10 metres) seemed to rule out the possibility of any life form being able to survive there. Some amazing specimens, however, can be found at depths of around 1000 metres, such as the deep-sea

The chimaera is a bottom-dweller which sometimes descends to depths of 2500 m.

The fish which inhabit the ocean depths often look like frightening monsters from another age or world.

▼ In order to attract prey or find a partner in the pitch-black waters of the ocean, some fish, such as the hatchet fish, emit light. This emission of light, known as bioluminescence, is caused by chemical substances secreted in their bodies. The distribution of these substances is different in every fish, creating a unique pattern of light for each individual. These patterns can also be produced by bacteria living in symbiosis with the fish. The phenomenon of bioluminescence also occurs out of water in fireflies and glow-worms.

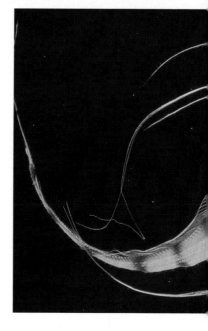

The deep-sea hatchet fish, with its bulging eyes, luminous scales and gaping jaws.

hatchet fish and the elongated oarfish, which has an extremely narrow body and a crown-like dorsal fin on its head. The rare specimens to be washed ashore so fired the imagination of fishermen and sailors that they believed that oarfish were 'kings' who guided herring and salmon during their migrations.

In the ocean depths

Deep-sea fish are generally small since food is rare at such depths. In order to survive, they have to be able to attract victims and be ready to gulp them down, regardless of their size. One specimen that does just that is the deep-sea angler fish which has been known to swallow prey larger then itself! It attracts the fish and various invertebrates that it feeds off by means of a 'fishing rod' on its head, formed by the foremost spine of its dorsal fin. Others, like the chimaera, prefer digging in the ocean bed to find molluscs and crustaceans which they crush with ease. There are very few fish below 3500 metres and none at all in the ocean trenches of the hadal regions (from the Greek *haides*, meaning hell), some 6000 metres below the surface.

Fish in
OUR
WORLD

It takes more than a spell of freezing winter weather to put off a keen angler. All you have to do is make a hole in the ice...and wait!

Fishing around the world

From the earliest fishing techniques used by prehistoric peoples to the Kevlar rods of today and the radar installed in modern fishing fleets, human beings have always shown a great deal of ingenuity when it comes to catching fish, either as a means of survival or simply for pleasure.

Mauritanian fishermen, who still fish using traditional methods, sort their catch on the beach as soon as they return from a fishing expedition.

Like hunting, fishing was practised by humans long before the days of farming or agriculture. A number of techniques of prehistoric origin are still used throughout the world and have not changed significantly over the millennia. In the South Pacific and the waters of South Asia, fishermen still dive into streams and catch fairly large fish with their bare hands. In Africa, spears and arrows continue to be used for fishing while in the Northern Hemisphere, a range of harpoons are still in everyday use.

In Peru, as in Europe, catfish are fished with a rod and line.

In Africa, the Nile perch is caught using spears and assegais. The rivers and lakes of Africa are some of the most densely populated in the world.

On the island of Madagascar, fish are driven into the shallows by people in the water where they are caught in traps similar to lobster pots.

In Japan, harpoon fishing is not just a male province.

A thousand and one ways of catching a fish

Early in the history of fishing, as they experimented with different ways of catching fish, people learned how to use poisons obtained from plants or lime to paralyse fish in lakes or slow-flowing rivers so that they could be plucked out of the water. In some regions, fish are still caught using traps similar to lobster pots or landing nets, placed in bottlenecks downstream of a waterfall or purpose-built dam. In other areas, small streams are blocked with heaps of reeds and people wade

Fish caught in African lakes, rivers and estuaries are an important source of protein and vitamins for the local communities.

The construction of a dam to prevent fish leaving a particular stretch of water is one of the oldest known techniques used in fishing.

into the water to chase the fish towards a shallow spot where they can be caught more easily.

Hook, line and sinker

People all over the world have been fishing with hooks tied to the end of lines for over 15,000 years, even though, among Eskimos for example, metal hooks have now replaced those originally made of bone or walrus tusk. Since time immemorial, fishermen have been expert in the art of setting fishing lines and using floats, sinkers and bait.

Fishermen throughout the world use nets to catch fish.

Fishing with a net...

In addition to rods, nets are also widely used. Some are fixed and channel the fish through a narrow passage which opens out into a bag at the end while others are moved around. Cast nets are thrown on the surface of the water and square dipping nets are repeatedly submerged and raised from the depths. Some nets are fitted with floats and sinkers and carried along by the current or tide. Others are drawn tight so that fish become caught in the mesh.

...or a kite!

Fishermen in the Solomon Islands have perfected an amazing method of fishing. First they gather spiders' webs and make them into a loop. This is attached with a line to the tail of a kite which the fisherman drags behind his canoe. The glistening web skims the surface of the water, attracting a particular species of garfish which gets its teeth caught in this ingenious trap.

The noble sport of fishing

Although many fishers earn a living by catching fish, many others fish purely for pleasure. It is said that the Roman emperors

In Siberia, people fish through the ice, sheltered by a hut built for this purpose.

The square dipping net is like a huge tablecloth held in position at each corner. It is submerged and then quickly raised to catch the fish swimming over it.

In China and Japan, cormorants have been domesticated and used for fishing for many centuries. At night, fishing boats head out on to the water, lit up with torches which are used to attract fish. The fishermen release ten or so cormorants, each wearing a collar attached to a line several metres long. The birds then dive into the water, catching fish which they store in a gular sac (throat pouch). When the birds return to the boat, the fishermen massage their necks to make them regurgitate the ten or so fish stored in each pouch.

Augustus and Nero were very keen fishermen and later, during the Middle Ages, fishing became a popular pastime for nobles and clerics in Europe.

The fisher's bible

The first treatise on angling, written by Dame Juliana Barnes, the daughter of an adviser to the King of England, was published in London in 1486. The book described the tying of twelve artificial flies, six of which are still used today. There is no doubt, however, that the most famous book on fishing is Isaac Walton's

Be careful when removing the hook! The pike's mouth is full of sharp teeth.

The fast-moving clear waters of mountain streams are the natural habitat of trout which often take refuge from the current in nooks and crannies.

The ultimate sport: game fishing is an unforgettable experience. The struggle to land a tuna or swordfish can sometimes last for hours.

The Compleat Angler (1653), of which there have been over 300 editions. Only the Bible itself has a more distinguished publishing record. This wealth of literature on fishing is a reflection of how popular the sport has remained in Britain.

Fishing for pleasure

Ever since the 17th century, the leisured classes in Britain have practised the gentlemanly sport of angling. Not only did these well-heeled devotees of the rod and line lay down the first rules governing fishing, but until the period between the two World Wars, the main technical improvements were also British in origin. Other nations were quick to follow. Today, millions of keen anglers in the western world fish for pleasure and strict regulations have had to be imposed as a result. Nowadays, fishing is not allowed without a permit or out of season and only approved equipment can be used since fish have dramatically decreased in numbers.

Angling competitions always attract large numbers of enthusiasts.

Herring wars

Commercial fishing, both offshore and in open waters, has also

In the tradition of the gentleman angler of the 18th century, some fly-fishers continue to practise their sport in style.

▼ The Chinese have farmed fish since ancient times and now produce over 3 million tonnes a year. The yield from pools where fish are fattened can be as much as 2 tonnes per hectare. In Europe, the reproductive cycle of the carp has been controlled since the Middle Ages and many fish are now farmed, to a greater or lesser extent, intensively. The reproductive cycle may be controlled entirely, as is the case with carp, trout and salmon, or partially by means of artificially induced spawning, hatcheries, fish fattening, etc.

undergone enormous expansion. For thousands of years, certain villages, regions and even entire nations specialized in fishing and their catches engendered the development of huge trade networks. As early as the Middle Ages, the Hanseatic League obtained the exclusive right to fish for herring off the coasts of Sweden and held a monopoly on transporting this merchandise all over Northern Europe where fish is an important foodstuff. The rise and fall of more than one sea-faring empire was connected with fishing. During the 17th century, Holland went to war in defence of

In the Maldives, commercial fishing still retains a traditional character.

For many years now, powerful hydraulic winches have been used to lift big fish, such as this tuna, on board fishing boats.

During the 11th century, in the Byzantine Empire, fishermen who went out by night frequently used torches and lamps to lure fish into their nets.

its right to fish off the coast of Scotland, only to be defeated by England, the future ruler of the waves.

Northern waters rich in fish

The fish population of the world is not evenly distributed throughout its oceans. This distribution depends upon complex food chains which encompass everything from micro-organisms to large predatory fish. The renewal of these food chains is governed by a number of factors, such as the different levels of nutrient salts

North-Sea fishermen landing on a beach during the 19th century.

Le Petit Journal

TOUS LES JOURS
Le Petit Journal
5 Centimes

SUPPLÉMENT ILLUSTRÉ
Huit pages : CINQ centimes

TOUS LES DIMANCHES
Le Supplément Illustré
5 Centimes

Cinquième Année   LUNDI 19 MARS 1894   Numéro 174

DÉPART DES PÊCHEURS D'ISLANDE

Articles on fishing regularly appeared in the pages of the world's press during the 19th century since, at that time, sailing on the high seas was fraught with risk and danger.

Fishermen's wives anxiously await the return of their husbands.

carried into the sea by large rivers (this has a particular effect on off-shore fish stocks), the meeting of warm and cold currents (such as occurs off Newfoundland) and rising currents created by the sunlight (on the west coast of America, for example). Ideal conditions are to be found above or in the immediate vicinity of the continental slopes which means that relatively few fish live in the open seas. Until recently, how-ever, 70% of the fish eaten in the world came from the extensive epicontinental seas of the Northern Hemisphere. Although

During the 19th century, fishing developed into a major industry. Enormous quantities of fish were cleaned and processed to supply large urban markets in Europe.

Trawlers with powerful engines and huge nets made of synthetic fibres have increased the yields of commercial fishing enormously.

▼ Driven by the need to supplement dwindling fish stocks in their own waters, the fishing fleets of the industrialized countries that dominate the world fishing industry (Russia, Japan and the European Union) are now fishing off Patagonia and Mauritania. In 1998, Mauritania agreed to allow EU fleets to fish in its territorial waters in exchange for financial aid. This has meant, however, that Mauritanian nationals have found themselves banned from fishing and are forced to buy sardines caught off their own coasts and tinned on European boats.

A thousand-metre trawl net is raised in open water.

an incredible variety of fish live in warm seas, the largest species, most sought after by fishermen, live in cold waters. Only about ten species make up one third of the hundred million tonnes of fish caught each year; some 70 species represent more than half of the fish eaten in the world.

The threat of overfishing

The technological revolution at the end of the 19th century completely changed the face of commercial fishing. Sails were abandoned in favour of engines, and nets increased in size and were hauled in using winches. Nowadays, large shoals are detected using radar and the volume of fish caught has increased considerably. Catches doubled every ten years between 1918 and 1970. Since then, over-fishing has exhausted fish stocks in many traditional fishing grounds. International measures, such as the imposition of quotas and temporary bans, have often had little effect faced with the determination of certain nations to continue fishing at all costs. In the 16th century, it was said of the fishing grounds off Newfoundland that a person could walk to shore on the backs of fish. Now, however, those days are long gone.

In hot countries, fish are preserved by drying and smoking. In Madagascar, jack fish are laid out on racks to dry in the sun and wind.

From the water to the table

Once caught, fish must be
prepared for immediate consumption
or preserved for future use by freezing,
salting, drying or smoking. More techniques
have been developed for preserving fish throughout
the world than for any other foodstuff.

The char, one of the most delicate-tasting freshwater fish, is a relative of the salmon.
It lives in cold lakes at high altitudes and is unfortunately becoming increasingly rare.

Whether caught in fresh water or out on the open sea, fish is a perishable foodstuff which must be consumed without delay. If it is not eaten immediately, then it must be preserved. The methods used to preserve fish are as old as fishing itself, varying from one region to another according to the local climate. In countries where the winters are cold, fish caught during the spring and summer months are stored in caves or pits dug in the frozen ground or surrounded by snow and crushed ice in thick-walled constructions made of earth.

Fresh fish must be transported quickly to market.

Shark fins are dried before being sold. They are an expensive rarity to which the Chinese attribute aphrodisiac properties.

Refrigeration is one of the oldest methods of preserving fish to be used in cold and temperate countries. Crushed ice is still used today in many parts of the world.

Sardines are hung up to dry under cover in Scandinavian countries.

Smoking, salting, drying ...

Another method of preserving fish is to dry it in the sun and open air – a technique much used in Africa – or in an enclosed space heated by fire. Fire is also used for smoking fish, a technique which is particularly popular in Europe, North America and Polynesia. Salting, often combined with drying and smoking, is less common, since for many years salt was a rare commodity in many areas. In the absence of salt, or if only a limited amount was available, fish was preserved by maceration, a technique which is

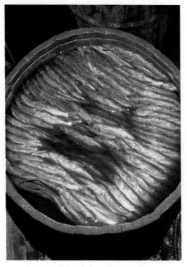

The process of maceration preserves the fish and enhances its flavour.

still used along the Pacific coasts, in Asia and North America. These different methods of preserving fish not only allowed fishermen to build up stocks for the seasons when it was not possible to fish, but also meant that they could transport their catch to distant markets in order to sell it.

The many faces of the herring...

In northern Europe, the herring has been a commodity of enormous significance for almost a thousand years. Herring fishing brought about the emergence of the

In Europe, the sardine is principally a spring and summer fish. It is dried beside the sea, as shown here in Portugal, so that it can then be eaten all year round.

Until recently, the herring was the most important sea fish caught for food and formed part of the staple diet for the working classes of northern Europe.

Hanseatic League, a mercantile association of Baltic and North-Sea towns, and prompted the drafting of the first rules of maritime law. For several centuries, the trade in herrings was as important as the spice trade. Furthermore, during the Middle Ages, the absence of herring from the market was an indication of food shortages. It was also used as a form of currency to pay ransoms and was even given as a gift. The church deemed it a suitable food to be eaten during Lent and on days when no meat could be eaten. In northern Europe, herring is still eaten in a

Herrings were used as a form of currency for several centuries.

great number of different forms, from cured herrings (hung up and smoked), salted herrings (which are preserved in barrels), bloaters (cured and lightly smoked herring) and rollmops or Baltic herrings (marinated in white wine) to buckling (salted for several hours then smoked) and kippers (smoked or salted split herrings which have long been a popular breakfast dish in Britain).

...and the cod

The cod is another tremendously important fish, which has been dried and eaten since Viking times. At the end of the Middle Ages, Norway supplied almost all of Europe with a type of cod which was known as 'stockfish' (air-dried on racks). Until recently in France, a distinction was made between cod caught for eating fresh and cod caught for salting on board ship. The cod is native to the coasts of the North Atlantic and for a long time was a staple foodstuff of great strategic importance since stores of cod meant that a town could survive a siege. Cod liver is used in 'brandade', a dish made of salt cod pounded with garlic, oil and cream. The haddock is a close relative of the cod and famous in its own right. It is often smoked.

In northern Europe, cod is often air-dried on racks.

The association of the fishmonger or fishwife with lower-class existence and coarse language has survived in a number of cultures.

▼ The Japanese are amongst the world's greatest consumers of fish, thanks to the extensive breeding grounds situated off their coasts. The most popular fish are the tuna ('bonito') and the sea bream which are eaten in the form of raw fillets or 'sushi' (small balls of rice and rolls of seaweed topped with fish and shellfish). Another great speciality is the 'fugu' or porcupine fish. This fish, whose organs contain a dangerous poison, is cleaned and prepared following a strict procedure by specially qualified chefs.

Tuna: from the sea to the tin

As far back as ancient times, tuna was extremely popular with Mediterranean peoples. The Phoenicians salted and smoked the fish and Greek texts describe the routes taken by shoals of migrating tuna off their islands. During the Middle Ages, tuna was cleaned, cut up, roasted, or fried in olive oil, and eaten with plenty of salt and spices. Tuna fish preserved in oil was to Mediterranean merchants what the barrel of salted herrings was to their northern counterparts. Until the end of the 19th century, small-

Fish was part of the staple diet in ancient Rome and appears on many frescoes.

Tuna is not just popular in the Mediterranean. This migratory fish is also highly prized by fishermen on the African side of the Indian Ocean.

In Sri Lanka and many other developing countries, small-scale coastal fishing still supplies the local markets with fresh fish.

Tuna is cut up on board as soon as it is caught, as shown on this Spanish boat.

scale tuna fishing persisted in many tiny ports where lookouts announced the arrival of the migrating fish. Nowadays, tuna is fished in the Atlantic where shoals are located by helicopters or satellites. Back in the shops, it is usually bought in tinned form.

Salmon: once more an affordable luxury

During the 19th century, salmon was still so plentiful in mainland Europe that servants had written in their contracts that they would not be given it to eat more than twice a week! The fish has now

Fennel is an aromatic herb used in Eastern Europe and Scandinavia to flavour salmon. It is oriental in origin and was introduced into Europe in ancient times.

Rainbow trout is highly prized for its tasty flesh.

disappeared from most European rivers and, until the 1960s, when salmon farming (raising young salmon in cages in the sea) brought it down in price, its scarcity made it a very costly meal. Wild salmon, which is generally considered to have a better taste, remains quite expensive.

Tinned sardines

The 19th century witnessed a revolution not only in fishing methods, but also in the way in which fish was preserved, marketed and eaten. Over in France, the Parisian chef and

Like these salmon caught in Alaska, a large proportion of the fish used to supply the markets of industrialized countries is sold in pieces, particularly in the form of fillets.

inventor Nicolas Appert discovered how to preserve food in hermetically sealed containers, whilst in Britain, the metal industry developed tin-plating techniques. These two inventions led to the opening of the first sardine canning factory in Nantes, on the coast of Brittany. Back in 1826, Joseph Colin was producing ten thousand tins a year; by 1880, production had already increased to 50 million. The tinned-salmon industry began in Scotland at about the same time while large-scale production of tinned fish on the west coast of the United States began in 1864.

In the Far East, the royal carp is farmed in the waters of the rice paddies.

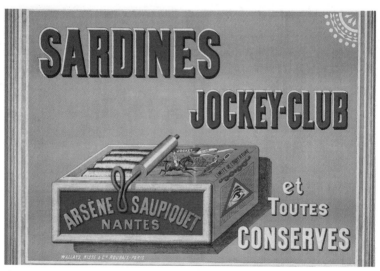

Sardines have been pressed and salted since the Middle Ages. The first sardine-canning factory, in Nantes in France, began production in 1824.

Enormous canning factories convert tonnes of tuna into the tinned fish found on supermarket shelves all over the world.

From chilled fish to frozen fish

As early as the beginning of the 19th century, fish was dispatched to far-off markets packed in crushed ice. It was, however, the rapid expansion of the railway system that enabled the fishing industry to supply consumers with fish at a reasonable price. New techniques of refrigeration, such as the production of artificial ice in blocks, the development of cold storage chambers and refrigerated trucks and ships, significantly increased the options available to the food industry. At the turn of

In China, shark fins are a delicacy used to make a particular type of soup.

Nowadays, cold storage starts in the hold of the fishing boat. As soon as the fish is caught, it is packed in ice in the hold.

▼ Almost as popular as the fish themselves are the eggs, or roe, of certain species. These are often smoked or salted before being eaten, and, in the case of lumpfish roe, artificially coloured red or black. Salted carp roe forms the basis of taramasalata, a pink Greek spread, but the most famous is undoubtedly caviar, the salted roe of the sturgeon found in the Caspian and Black seas. There are three different grades (beluga, osetrova and sevruga) which sell for between £600 and £1500 a kilo, depending on their quality.

the century, fast-freezing techniques and the development of long-term cold storage made it possible to keep fish for much longer periods. These new techniques also meant that the oldest methods of preserving fish were used less: in industrialized countries, fresh or frozen fish is now preferred to salted, smoked or dried fish.

Fast-freezing techniques mean that fish can be kept for much longer periods.

Changing diets

The rise in living standards, at least in the Western world, means that meat has eclipsed fish in popularity. It is no longer only eaten by the rich, or saved for special occasions and is now available to a wider public. Even in Britain, fish and chips, for a long time the most popular take-away food, currently faces competition from other types of fast food. In addition to these social trends, overfishing has also pushed up the price of many types of fish. Today it is the nutritional value of fish that is used to promote sales. Being rich in minerals, trace elements and vitamins as well as fatty acids it is recommended not only as part of a well-balanced diet but also as a way to reduce levels of cholesterol.

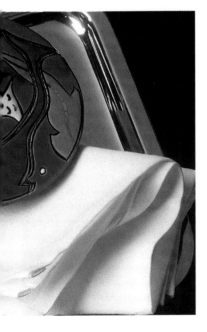

No other species epitomizes the domestication of fish more than *Carassius auratus*, more commonly known as the goldfish.

Fish behind glass

Fascinated by the colours and shapes found in the world's oceans, people have long sought to recreate this aquatic environment in their own homes. From goldfish in a simple bowl to exotic specimens in large and sophisticated aquariums, our 'finned friends' continue to delight young and old alike.

In a salt-water aquarium, it is possible to recreate the natural environment of a tropical reef in all its splendour, right down to the tiniest details.

T he *Carassius auratus*, more commonly known by the generic name of goldfish, is closely related to the carp but is distinguished from the latter by its lack of barbels. Both species have been selectively bred by humans for centuries.

The goldfish in China

A Chinese chronicle dating from the Song dynasty (960–1120 AD) makes an early reference to the breeding of a kind of goldfish in natural pools. During the centuries that followed, these finned creatures became popular at the

The first goldfish were exported from China to Japan in around 1500 AD.

This still life by Paula Modersohn-Becker (1876–1907) bears witness to the great popularity of goldfish in European homes at the end of the 19th century.

The temporary aquarium set up during the Paris World Fair in 1867 attracted huge crowds, curious to discover the fascinating world beneath the sea.

Selective breeding has produced many different shapes and colours of goldfish.

imperial court and with the nobility. The fashion then spread throughout China since goldfish could be kept just as well in clay tubs as in more regal jade tanks.

Artificial selection

By cross-breeding fish with the desired characteristics, the Chinese succeeded in creating a number of varieties. At first this selective breeding concentrated on colour but gradually it encompassed shape as well. Fins disappeared, increased in size or changed in appearance, and varieties with strange bulging eyes, warty skin and pearly scales appeared. The endless inventiveness of the Chinese breeders is reflected in the names of varieties such as the 'veiltail' (with a three-lobed flowing tail), the 'celestial' (with protruding upward-directed eyes) and the 'lionhead' (with a swollen hood-like growth on its head).

Goldfish in a bowl

The goldfish was exported to Europe during the 17th century and quickly became popular with the aristocracy as a decorative feature in a glass bowl on a table. Like most things, goldfish went in and out of fashion and were at the height of their popularity at the beginning of the 20th century. Some owners, who grew tired of keeping goldfish, released them into the wild where they can still be found in fresh and slightly salt water, having returned to their natural state and colour which is not gold but grey.

In the 20th century, the aquarium became a decorative feature in people's homes.

The fascination of the world beneath the sea

In 1853, the first public aquarium opened in London's Regent's Park. As large sheets of specially manufactured thick glass became

Specialist shops now offer several thousand species of fish for aquarium enthusiasts. The goldfish, however, is still the most widely kept species.

▼ Since the 1920s and 30s, many groups of enthusiasts have organized fish exhibitions and competitions. Tropical fish are the most sought-after since the range of colours is enormous and many fish can be kept together in a confined space without them eating each other. Most of these fish are bred specially for aquariums but in response to the enormous demand, several rare species have been poached from the wild and, as a result, are today threatened with extinction.

The impressive public aquarium in the zoological gardens in Berlin was one of the first to be built in Europe.

Fish shows are organized for many different species, including carp.

increasingly available, other cities were able to follow suit and build their own aquariums. Among the first opened were those in Berlin (1869), Naples (1873) and Paris (1878). Jules Verne's novel *Twenty Thousand Leagues Under the Sea* (1870) offered readers a literary glimpse of the mysterious underwater world at the same time as these public aquariums were being built to allow people to explore the deeps without leaving the city. Soon, people began buying smaller aquariums to have in their own homes.

Sophisticated technology, including tempered glass, pumps, artificial lighting and controlled water temperature, is needed to recreate a miniature tropical world in an aquarium.

The 16th-century Italian artist Giuseppe Arcimboldo drew a great deal of inspiration from fish and other sea creatures when creating his strange figures.

Fish symbols and legends

Rock drawings in Australia, tribal masks in Africa, tile mosaics in ancient Rome, ceremonial robes in South America...wherever there is water, people have always been inspired by fish. Adopted by Christians as a symbol of their religion, fish also form the lower half of those curious creatures of mythology, the sirens.

Cave drawings in the Kakadu National Park in Australia depict the aboriginal story of the Creation, including the appearance of the first fish.

I n the Old Testament, no distinction is drawn between the various creatures that inhabit water, except for one reference: those lacking scales or fins are considered impure and people are prohibited from eating them. Elsewhere, other biblical stories refer to fish and fishing in a symbolic way.

In the belly of the fish

The best-known story involving a fish is probably that of Jonah. Having been sent by God to Nineveh to warn the city's sinful inhabitants of the divine

Fish were frequently used as a decorative motif in the mosaics of pagan Rome.

Even though we now know the story as Jonah and the whale, the original version describes how the prophet was swallowed by a large fish.

During the first centuries AD, the fish and the lamb were widely used as symbols of Christ on tombstones in Christian catacombs.

Jesus recruits his first disciples, the fishermen Simon and Andrew.

punishment awaiting them, the prophet tried to avoid his mission by fleeing on a ship. A great storm arose and, fearing the wrath of God, the sailors cast Jonah into the sea whereupon the waters immediately became calm again. Jonah was swallowed by a huge fish and spent three days and three nights in its belly before his prayers were finally answered and the fish spat him forth again so that he could accomplish his task. Due to a poor translation from the original Greek, the large fish that swallowed Jonah is now generally thought of as a whale.

Christ Walking on the Water (1444) by Konrad Witz is the first painting to depict an identifiable landscape (Lake Geneva). In this scene, fishermen are shown at work on the lake.

Bread and fish formed the basis of the daily diet in Palestine at the time of Christ. According to some traditions, Jesus and the Apostles ate fish at the last supper.

The miracle of the fishes

The New Testament accords fishing a special significance. According to the Gospel of St Matthew, Jesus met his first disciples Simon (called Peter) and his brother Andrew beside the Sea of Galilee. He called to them: 'Follow me and I will make you fishers of men'. And they left their nets and followed him. In St Luke's version of the same story, this conversion of the future Apostles is preceded by a miracle. Jesus told the poor fishermen who had just spent the night on the lake

Jupiter, the king of the gods, depicted with Pisces (the sign of the Fish).

without catching a single fish to 'put forth' and cast their nets again. They caught so many fish that the boat almost sank beneath their weight. Fishing also figures in several parables. Jesus compared the fisherman sorting the fish caught in his net to the angels who will separate the just from the unjust on the Day of Judgement.

The fish as a symbol of Christ

It is probably for this reason that, in the early Christian art of the first centuries AD, Jesus is often represented by a hook holding two fish. The fish itself is also used as a symbol of Christ since the initials of the formula 'Jesus Christ, Son of God, Saviour' form the Greek word 'ichthus' meaning 'fish'. Other representations show a ship on the back of a fish, symbolizing Christ carrying the church. This tradition died out during the 4th century when Greek was replaced by Latin in the Church.

Days of abstinence

From the first half of the 6th century onwards, Benedictine monks did not merely content themselves with observing the rule of celibacy and the fasts

A Triton adorns Pietro Tacca's baroque fountain (1629) in Florence.

This illustration from a 15th-century German Bible shows how artists often introduced extraneous characters, such as these mermaids, into their portrayals of biblical tales.

▼ Poseidon, the ancient Greek god of the sea and rivers, is usually depicted with an escort of Tritons, strange creatures that are half-man, half-fish, with scaly bodies, fins on their stomachs and chests and a double fish tail instead of legs. This mythological tradition, which was adopted by the Romans for their sea god Neptune (pictured left), perhaps influenced later representations of sirens or mermaids.
During the Baroque period (17th century), Tritons were often depicted on fountains.

which punctuate the Christian calendar. They also abstained from eating the flesh of four-legged animals. Several centuries later, the laity adopted this practice once a week with the result that many people ate fish, particularly of the salted variety, on a Friday.

Bewitching sirens

In the Middle Ages, strange creatures with the upper body of a woman and the sinuous scaly tail of a fish instead of legs began to appear on the capitals of churches and monasteries. The

Odysseus tied to the mast of his ship while the sirens sing.

A 12th-century painting of a mermaid on the ceiling of the church of St Martin in Zillis, Switzerland. She is depicted as playing a horn instead of singing her bewitching song.

Since ancient times, the siren or mermaid has been depicted as a seductive woman luring her victims to their death, as shown in this 19th-century engraving.

Sadko, the rich merchant of a Russian epic, in the realm of the mermaids.

name given to these mysterious women of the sea, sirens, dates back to ancient Greece. Homer describes how Odysseus makes his companions tie him to the mast of the ship and cover their own ears as they sail past the sirens so that they do not succumb to the nymphs' bewitching song and allow themselves to be lured on to the rocks. However, the poet is silent on the subject of their appearance and representations on Greek vases depict the sirens as having wings! In the Christian imagination, mermaids retain

Every era has created its own images of the mermaid. This work by Robert Anning Bell (1900) is inspired by the ideal of beauty popularized by the English Pre-Raphaelites.

Melusina's husband realized he had married a nymph when he saw her bathing.

their bewitching nature, but are seen as luring the faithful towards a shipwreck of a more spiritual kind. According to an Irish legend, a mermaid called out to St Columba when he was spreading the word of God on the island of Iona. She fell in love with him and asked him to give her his soul. He resisted and demanded that she come out of the sea. The mermaid refused but, before disappearing, shed tears which fell as pebbles... Some pictures show sailors seduced by the physical beauty of the mermaids rather than by their

Illuminated texts often depict mermaids and other fantastic creatures as in this title page to the Book of Esther in a Hebrew manuscript.

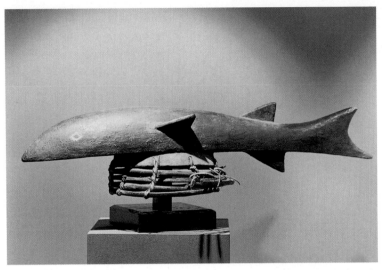

This helmet originally belonging to a member of the Ijo people from Nigeria is adorned with a stylized fish, reflecting a time when their economy was primarily based on fishing.

At the end of the 16th century, Charles IX of France issued a decree moving the start of the year, which until then had been 1 April, back to 1 January. The tradition of giving gifts to mark the 'old' New Year has persisted in France to this day in the form of sham presents and hoax messages on April 1. Since the sun leaves the zodiac sign of Pisces (the Fish) at the end of March, these April Fools' tricks are known as 'poissons d'avril' (April fish). Fish made of marzipan, sugar and chocolate are sold all over France on that day.

Fish and birds adorn this ceremonial poncho from Peru.

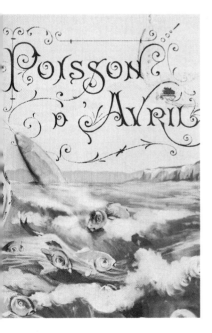

singing. Mermaids are sometimes depicted with wings and claws and sometimes – in the form that we now recognize – with fishes' tails. By the time of the Renaissance, the mermaid had become a symbol of eloquence and erudition and still continues to exert a certain fascination. In Shakespeare's *A Midsummer Night's Dream*, a mermaid seated on the back of a dolphin sings an enchanting song.

A tragic tale

At the beginning of the 19th century, it was the turn of the German Romantics to succumb to the charms of the siren, or rather her Germanic counterpart who sat on the Lorelei rock above the Rhine singing to lure sailors to their deaths. Inspired by the novel *Undine* (1811) by the German writer La Motte-Fouqué, Hans Christian Andersen transformed the mermaid into a tragic character. In his book *The Little Mermaid*, the youngest daughter of the sea king wishes to marry a human prince. She trades her beautiful voice for a witch's brew in order to change her fish's tail into legs, but all in vain. The prince marries another and the unhappy mermaid disappears back into the spume.

FISH

star animals

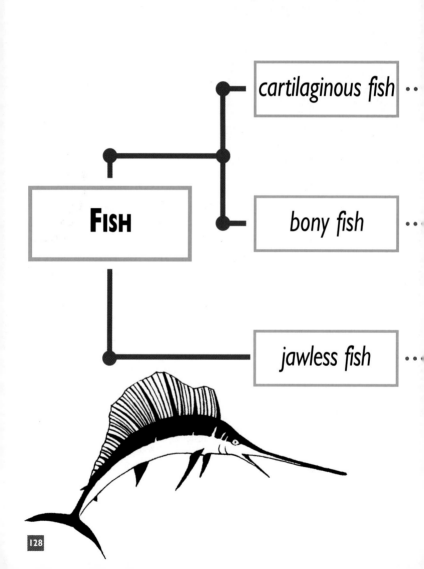

cartilaginous fish ··

bony fish ··

jawless fish ··

There are several hundred species of shark, all of them feared predators, but only about 20 pose any threat to humans.

The manta ray sucks in huge quantities of water which it filters through its comb-like gill slits.

Some lunged fish await the rainy season in a cocoon buried in the ground, taking in oxygen from the air.

The lamprey has a jawless sucking mouth which it attaches to other fish, feeding on their blood as a parasite.

The seahorse is classed as a fish even though it does not look much like one. Its courtship dance is a veritable ballet.

The river trout lives in mountain streams and is highly prized as a game and food fish.

Creative Workshop

*Having studied all of these creatures,
it's time to get creative.*

*All you need are a few odds and ends and a
little ingenuity, and you can incorporate
some of the fish we've seen into
beautiful craft objects.*

*These simple projects will give you further
insight into the world of fish presented in
the pages of this book.*

*An original and simple way to enjoy the wonderful
images of the world of fish.*

Mosaic tidy

C urved patterns are perfectly suited to mosaic work.
The small squares in this particular design create a
swirling background on
which the fish twists
and turns.

Preparation
• Sketch the
design of the fish
onto the bottom of
the terracotta tray.
• Cut the green and
brown ceramic tiles into
small squares using the
pliers. Protect your eyes while
cutting the mosaic pieces by wearing
suitable goggles.

Building the mosaic
• Stick the mosaic pieces onto the
design with tile glue, using light
brown pieces for the head, dark
brown for the backbone and several
shades of green for the rest of the
body.
• Shape three dark blue pieces of tile
into circles to form the bubbles.

Fill in the background around the design with pieces of light grey and light blue tile. Using similar size pieces in dark blue, form an initial border around the edge of the tray, then in two shades of green, cut slightly larger pieces to form a second border.

The cement

• Wait 24 hours for the glue to dry, then prepare the grout as indicated in the

manufacturer's instructions. Spread it over the mosaic using a palette knife, filling all the gaps and taking care to cover the raised edges of the pot.

• Before the grout has

set, remove the excess with a damp sponge.
• Leave to dry for one hour, then polish with a dry cloth.
• Use the tray for keeping loose change or keys in.

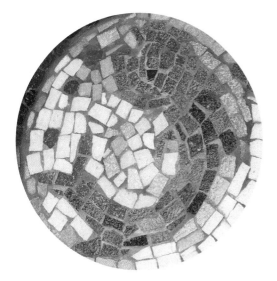

Materials

• a terracotta plantpot tray, 16 cm in diameter
• heavy-duty pliers to cut the mosaic pieces
• a soft-leaded pencil
• a tube of tile glue
• a pot of brown grout for tiles
• a palette knife.
• a sponge
• ceramic tiles in several shades of dark and light green, blue, grey and brown
• a pair of plastic goggles

Fish jewellery

O n the shelves of your local fishing tackle shop you will find some wonderful spinners and lures. The strangest and most original ones can be used to make novel pieces of jewellery, such as these earrings and brooch.

The fish

• Use the pliers to remove all the hooks attached to the spinner.

• Sketch three fins and three tails onto the sheet brass using a pencil. Cut out the shapes and etch lines on to each one with a ballpoint pen as shown.

• Use the awl to pierce a small hole at the end of each piece and attach them to the rings on the tail and belly of the fish with wire.

• Slide a piece of wire 10 cm long into the

earring hooks, fold in two, then thread the beads onto the wire. Attach the wire to the ring at the end of each fish's mouth.

The brooch

• Attach a length of wire in the same way to the ring at the mouth of the largest fish. Add a small bead at the end.

• Trace the wave design on to the sheet brass, cut it out and planish the surface gently with a hammer.

• Use superglue to attach the fish to the wave and to attach the pin to the back of the wave.

Materials

• 2 identical fish-shaped spinners or lures, and 1 slightly larger to make the brooch
• 20 small gilded beads and a few glass or wooden beads • a pair of earring hooks • 1 brooch pin • a piece of sheet brass that can be cut with scissors
• jewellery-making wire • pliers • a hammer • an awl • superglue • a ballpoint pen
• scissors

Flying fish table mat

This gold and silver flying fish will bring a touch of the sea to your table.

The design
• Photocopy the fish design shown here, enlarging it to 34 cm in length.
• Place the photocopy onto the work surface to use as a guide for shaping and assembling the pieces of wire.

The frame
• Cut 1.10 m of aluminium wire. Shape it into a fish (starting with the gill then forming the head, back, tail, belly, head again and the first dorsal fin), threading on 7 beads as shown.

The head and fins
• Twist the brass wire around the head,

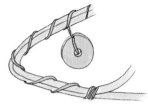

sliding the largest bead onto it and suspending it 1 cm from the top of the frame to form the eye.

• Use the aluminium wire to shape the second dorsal fin and the two ventral fins. Slide the last two beads onto this wire, and attach it to the frame using the brass wire.

The finishing touches

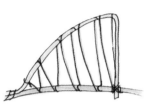

• Slide a bead onto the gill and use a length of brass wire to form the backbone, stretching from the tip of the gill to the end of the tail. Attach another bead to the gill on top of the brass wire.

• Use superglue to fix these two beads in place.

• Wind the brass wire around the body, the fins and the tail in a zigzag fashion.

Materials

• 1.5 m of 2 mm aluminium wire • 5 m of 0.5 mm brass wire • 10 coloured glass beads with a hole wide enough to thread onto the aluminium wire • 1 larger bead for the eye • superglue

Seaside mobile

With a couple of lampshades, a few shells and some paper fish, you can create this attractive mobile to light your room.

The fish

• Photocopy the design of the fish twice, enlarging it to 18 cm in length.

• Cut the cardboard into four and divide the pieces into two, placing one piece on top of the other. Stick a photocopied fish on top of each pair using tape. Make sure that they remain firmly attached together while cutting out the shapes.

• Cut out the fish shapes with a Stanley knife, following the outline of the photocopies. Use a hole punch to form each fish's eye.

• Cover each fish on both sides with the blue spray paint before spraying them lightly and unevenly with the silver paint.

The eyelets

• Place eight eyelets at regular intervals around the bottom of each lampshade. Paint a wave design onto each.

Attaching the decoration

• Carefully pierce each shell with the awl. Attach shells around the shades by threading a length of wire through the hole in each shell, bending the wire over and twisting the two halves together.

• Slide a bead on to the wire so that it sits on top of the shell. Attach the shells and beads to the shade by threading the wire through the eyelets and bending the end over.

Assembly

• Attach 4 large and 4 small shells onto the lower shade, and 4 fish and 4 shells onto the upper one.

• Fix the lampshades to the light cable. Pass both shades onto the cable, fixing the lower shade in the normal position and allowing the other shade to rest on top.

Materials

• 2 lampshades of the same size, 1 for a lamp and 1 for hanging from the ceiling • blue and green fabric paint • a large paint brush • 20 gilded eyelets • pliers • fuse wire • 8 cockleshells and 4 smaller shells • 16 blue or green glass beads • an A3 sheet of thick cardboard • blue and silver spray paint • a hole punch • glue • a Stanley knife • an awl

Picture credits

Acknowledgements

The publishers would like to thank all those who have contributed
to the preparation of this book, in particular:

Guy-Claude Agboton, Angie Allison, Rupert Hasterok, Nicolas Lemaire,
Hervé Levano, Mike Mayor, Kha Luan Pham, Marie-Laure Ungemuth

Creative Workshop:
Evelyne-Alice Bridier (p. 132-133), Michèle Forest (p. 134-139)

Translation: Patricia Clarke, Sara Montgomery

Illustrations: Franz Rey

Printed in Italy
Eurolitho - Milan
May 1999